NAHB-OSHA

SCAFFOLD SAFETY HANDBOOK *English-Spanish*

GUIA DE SEGURIDAD *Española Inglesa* DEL ANDAMIO

NATIONAL ASSOCIATION OF HOME BUILDERS

NAHB–OSHA Scaffold Safety Handbook

BuilderBooks, a Service of the National Association of Home Builders

Elizabeth M. Rich	Director of Book Publishing
Doris M. Tennyson	Senior Editor
Marvyn Bacigalupo	Translator
Matthew Geiss	Illustrator
E Design Communications	Composition
McNaughton & Gunn	Printing

Gerald M. Howard	NAHB Executive Vice President and CEO
Mark Pursell	NAHB Senior Staff Vice President, Marketing & Sales Group
Lakisha Campbell	NAHB Staff Vice President, Publications & Affinity Programs

ISBN-13: 978-0-86718-574-4
ISBN-10: 0-86718-574-0

© 2004 by BuilderBooks™
of the National Association of Home Builders
of the United States of America

Printed in the United States of America

Library of Congress Cataloging-in-Publication Data

Scaffold safety handbook.—English-Spanish ed.
  p. cm.
 ISBN-13: 978-0-86718-574-4
 ISBN-10: 0-86718-574-0
 1. Scaffolding—Safety measures.

 TH5281.S273 2003
 690'.22—dc22

                      2003017580

Disclaimer
This publication is designed to provide accurate and authoritative information in regard to the subject matter covered. It is sold with the understanding that the publisher is not engaged in rendering legal, accounting, or other professional service. If legal advice or other expert assistance is required, the services of a competent professional person should be sought.

Esta publicación no contiene opiniones legales. La información aquí incluida es con el propósito de informar y servir como una base de instrucción para los empleadores a que instruyan a sus empleados sobre cuestiones de seguridad. Las casos pueden variar tremendamente, de modo que si lo desean, los empleadores pueden consultar con un abogado antes de actuar sobre las premisas aquí incluidas. Los constructores deben decidir por su propia cuenta cuales de los procedimientos y condiciones del programa protegerán mejor sus intereses.   —From a Declaration of Principles jointly adopted by a Committee of the American Bar Association and a Committee of Publishers and Associations.

For further information, please contact:

National Association of Home Builders
1201 15th Street, NW
Washington, DC 20005-2800
Check us out online at: www.BuilderBooks.com

Labor, Safety & Health Services at the National Association of Home Builders

The National Association of Home Builders (NAHB) is a Washington, D.C.-based trade association representing more than 205,000 members involved in home building, remodeling, multifamily construction, property management, subcontracting, design, housing finance, building product manufacturing and other aspects of residential and light commercial construction.

NAHB's Labor Safety & Health Services is committed to educating America's builders about the importance of construction safety. Our safety and health resources are designed to help builders control unsafe conditions, operate safe jobsites, comply with OSHA regulations and reduce their workers' compensation costs.

Occupational Safety and Health Administration

The mission of the Occupational Safety and Health Administration (OSHA) is to save lives, prevent injuries, and protect the health of America's workers. To accomplish this, federal and state governments must work in partnership with the more than 100 million working men and women and their six and a half million employers who are covered by the Occupational Safety and Health Act of 1970.

The National Association of Home Builders (NAHB) and OSHA recognize the value of establishing collaborative relationships to ensure safer and healthier worksites. NAHB and OSHA formed an Alliance to use their collective expertise and efforts to foster a culture of injury prevention and promote safe and healthful working conditions. Under the Alliance, NAHB and OSHA have been working together to provide important safety and health information to those in the residential construction industry.

Acknowledgments

A special acknowledgment for those individuals who assisted in the development of *Scaffold Safety Handbook, English-Spanish.* Special thanks are due to Alan Kline, President of Lynn Ladder and Scaffolding Co, Inc.; Steve C. Cloutier, Directorate of Construction at the Occupational Safety and Health Administration; Bob Woodward, Safety Environmental Engineering, Inc., Bob Masterson, Ryland Homes; Amanda Fisher and everyone at JLG Industries, Inc.

Special thanks to the Construction Safety and Health Committee and safety experts Robert Matuga, Director, NAHB Labor, Safety, and Health Services and George Middleton, Program Manager, Labor, Safety, and Health Services for their contribution to *Scaffold Safety Handbook, English-Spanish,* as well as their service and dedication to safety education in the homebuilding industry.

We also express our appreciation to the following for generous contributions of time and professional expertise in helping create this book: Tom McGonegal at Safeway Steel Products, Inc.; Steve Ashley at Rite-Way Concepts, Inc; Bob Barrish at Qual-Craft Industries, Inc.; Paul Riley at WallWalker, LLC; Brad G. Chisler at EdgeMoore Homes; Jeff B. Moore at Green Village Concrete, Inc.; Marko Kaar at Operation Safe Site; Marvyn Bacigalupo, American Translators Association Accredited Translator and managing editor of *El Nuevo Constructor*; and a special thanks to photographers Morris Semiatin and Shelly Harrison.

Contents

Indices

Introduction

Scaffolds can provide a safer and more efficient way to work in home building and remodeling. Every time a scaffold is erected, used, or dismantled it must be properly set up and certain protocols must be followed.

Even though the Occupational Safety and Health Administration (OSHA) has implemented and updated a scaffold safety standard, scaffold-related accidents that result in injuries and deaths continue to occur. OSHA estimates more than 9,000 injuries a year are related to working on or around scaffolds. At least 79 deaths each year are caused by unsafe scaffold use and according to data from the Department of Labor's Bureau of Labor Statistics (BLS) Census of Fatal Occupational Injuries, scaffold falls cause more than 3,000 disabling injuries each year.

Scaffold violations that were most frequently cited by OSHA in 2002:

- **No guardrails on scaffolds.** Consistently a problem with all types of scaffolds. More prevalent with smaller employers because equipment has not been purchased or rented with guardrails. Manufacturers will sell guardrails with metal scaffolds rented or sold. Many construction sites have been inspected after an OSHA compliance officer observed this condition in passing on the street.

- **Defective wood planks and inadequate planking overhang.** This is becoming an increasing citation item as more OSHA inspectors are investigating the planks for rot, saw marks, and cracks through the whole board. They are also observing the proper overlap and overhang of the planks.

- **Unsafe access to scaffold.** This occurs on sites that often do not have guardrail protection. Instead of providing stairs or ladder, many employers require the em-

Introducción

Los andamios pueden facilitar una manera más segura y eficaz de trabajar en la construcción y remodelación residencial. Cada vez que se monta, utiliza o desmonta un andamio se debe preparar correctamente y se deben seguir ciertos protocolos.

Si bien la Administración de Seguridad y Salud Ocupacional (OSHA) ha puesto en práctica y ha actualizado una norma de seguridad para andamios, continúan ocurriendo accidentes relacionados con los andamios que resultan en lesiones y muertes. La OSHA calcula que anualmente se producen más que 9,000 lesiones relacionadas con el trabajo sobre andamios o en su proximidad. Por lo menos 79 muertes cada año son el resultado del empleo poco seguro de los andamios y, según los datos del censo sobre lesiones ocupacionales mortales del Departamento de Estadísticas Laborales del Departamento del Trabajo (BLS), las caídas de andamios causaron más que 3,000 lesiones incapacitantes cada año.

Las reglas más quebrantadas en cuanto al uso de andamios citadas por la OSHA en 2002 son:

- **Falta de barandales de seguridad en los andamios.** Un problema constante con toda clase de andamios. Más frecuente entre empresas pequeñas a causa de qué no compran ni alquilan el equipo con barandales de seguridad. Los fabricantes venden barandales de seguridad con los andamios (comprados o alquilados). Muchas obras de construcción han sido inspeccionadas luego de que un inspector de la OSHA observó ese problema al pasar por la calle y lo reportó.

- **Tablones defectuosos y voladizo insuficiente de los mismos.** Esto cada vez se vuelve una multa más frecuente pues un mayor número de inspectores de la OSHA está investigando los tablones a lo ancho y a lo largo para determinar si tienen pudrición, marcas de sierra o fisuras. También se fijan si los tablones tienen voladizo suficiente y si están correctamente traslapados.

- **Acceso peligroso al andamio.** Esto ocurre en obras que a menudo no tienen barandales de seguridad. En lugar de proporcionar una escalera o peldaños, muchos empleadores

ployee to climb the cross brace or scaffold frames. This is a fall hazard. Many scaffold frames were not designed as ladders and the scaffold may tip over from side loading.

- **Cross bracing not adequate.** Manufacturers of scaffolds will require full cross bracing on all sections. Cross bracing can be used, in some instances, for partial guardrail requirements. (See General Requirements Section).

The contents of this booklet highlights the most common types of scaffolding found in residential construction today and references some of the major requirements for safely working on and around scaffolds. It is a quick reference guide and should not be used solely for the purposes of regulatory compliance. For detailed information, the Code of Federal Regulations for Scaffolds (29 CFR Part 1926 Subpart L) should be reviewed in its entirety. For further information see, OSHA's Publication, *A Guide to Scaffold Use in the Construction Industry*. If applicable, see the regulations pertaining to your state Occupational Safety and Health program.

le exigen al empleado que se trepe por las riostras o armazón del andamio. Eso es un peligro de caída. Muchos armazones de andamio no están diseñados para ser utilizados como escaleras y el andamio se podría caer a causa de la carga lateral.

● **Las riostras no son adecuadas.** Los fabricantes de andamios exigirán riostras en forma completa en todas las secciones. En algunos casos se pueden utilizar riostras para cumplir con el requisito de barandales parciales. (Consulte la sección de Requisitos generales).

En este folleto se hace hincapié sobre los tipos más comunes de andamios que se utilizan en la actualidad en la construcción de residencias y se citan algunos de los requisitos principales para trabajar sin peligro sobre andamios y en su proximidad. Se trata tan sólo de una guía de consulta y no debe utilizarse como medio único de referencia para los fines de cumplimiento con las normas. Para obtener información detallada corresponde consultar en su totalidad el Código de Reglamentos Federales para Andamios (29 CFR Part 1926 Subpart L). Para más información, consulte la publicación *A Guide to Scaffold Use in the Construction Industry* (Una guía para el empleo de andamios en la industria de la construcción) de OSHA. Si corresponde, consulte los reglamentos pertinentes del programa de Seguridad y Salud Ocupacional de su estado.

Training Requirements

Workers must be trained on the hazards of scaffolds before erecting, using, modifying, moving, or dismantling them.

Requisitos de Capacitación

Los trabajadores deben recibir adiestramiento sobre los peligros de los andamios antes de armarlos, usarlos, modificarlos, trasladarlos o desarmarlos.

Working on Scaffold

All workers who will be *using* scaffolds must be trained by a *qualified person* who is able to recognize and minimize scaffold hazards.

The training must include safe work practices for:

☑ Electrical Hazards
☑ Fall Protection Systems
☑ Falling Object Protection Systems
☑ Proper Usage of Scaffolds
☑ Materials Handling on Scaffolds
☑ Load-Carrying Capacities

Competent person. A competent person is capable of identifying existing and predictable hazards in the surroundings or working conditions which are unsanitary, hazardous, or dangerous to employees. A competent person is authorized by the employer to take prompt corrective measures to eliminate the unsafe working conditions.

Qualified person. A qualified person has earned a recognized degree, certificate or professional standing, or who by extensive knowledge, training, and experience, has successfully demonstrated the ability to solve or resolve problems related to the subject matter, the work, or the project.

El Trabajo en un Andamio

Todos los trabajadores que *utilizarán* andamios deberán ser adiestrados por una *persona calificada* capaz de reconocer y minimizar los peligros de los andamios.

La capacitación deberá incluir prácticas de seguridad en el trabajo sobre:

☑ Peligros eléctricos
☑ Sistemas de protección contra caídas
☑ Sistemas de protección contra objetos en caída
☑ Uso correcto de los andamios
☑ Manejo de materiales en un andamio
☑ Capacidad de carga

Persona competente. Una persona competente es capaz de identificar los peligros existentes y previsibles en el entorno y las situaciones de trabajo insalubres, arriesgadas o peligrosas para los empleados. Una persona competente está autorizada por el empleador para tomar medidas correctivas oportunas a fin de eliminar las situaciones de trabajo peligrosas.

Persona calificada. Una persona calificada es aquella que posee un título, certificado o posición profesional, o quien, por sus amplios conocimientos, capacitación y experiencia ha demostrado satisfactoriamente su aptitud para resolver o solucionar problemas relacionados con el asunto, trabajo u obra en cuestión.

Erecting and Dismantling Scaffold

In addition, training by a *competent person* must be given to workers who erect, dismantle, move, operate, repair, maintain, and inspect scaffolds.

The training must include safe work practices for:

☑ Erecting
☑ Dismantling
☑ Moving
☑ Operating
☑ Repairing
☑ Maintenance
☑ Inspecting

Workers must be re-trained if they lack the necessary safe work practice skills for erecting, using, or dismantling scaffolds.

Retraining also is required when workers are exposed to new hazards on the job, such as a change in the type of scaffold being used, changes in the use of a scaffold fall protection system or falling object protection system or when workers show signs of not knowing how to work safely.

Montaje y Desmontaje de un Andamio

Además, una *persona competente* debe capacitar a los trabajadores que montan, desmontan, trasladan, operan, reparan, mantienen e inspeccionan los andamios.

La capacitación deberá incluir prácticas de seguridad en el trabajo sobre:

- ☑ Montaje
- ☑ Desmontaje
- ☑ Traslado
- ☑ Operación
- ☑ Reparación
- ☑ Inspección
- ☑ Mantenimiento

Los trabajadores deberán tomar el curso otra vez si no poseen las aptitudes de seguridad necesarias para montar, usar o desmontar andamios.

También tendrá que volver a capacitarse el trabajador expuesto a nuevos peligros en el trabajo, como un cambio en el tipo de andamio que utiliza, cambios en el sistema de protección contra caídas de los andamios o el sistema de protección contra objetos en caída o cuando el trabajador muestre señales de no saber cómo trabajar sin correr peligro.

General Requirements

The scaffold standard requires that only a *competent person* be allowed to evaluate and/or train for certain tasks. Scaffolds can only be erected, moved, dismantled, or altered under the supervision and direction of a competent person.

Requisitos Generales

La norma sobre andamios dispone que sólo se le puede permitir a una *persona competente* evaluar y adiestrar para ciertas tareas. Los andamios podrán ser montados, trasladados, desmontados o alterados únicamente bajo la supervisión y dirección de una persona competente.

Capacity

Each scaffold must be capable of supporting its own weight and at least 4 times the expected load. The expected load includes workers, equipment, tools, and materials.

This section applies to scaffolds often used in the residential construction industry unless stated otherwise. Before building scaffolds, review all sections of the regulation to be sure you are following OSHA's requirements.

SCAFFOLD PLATFORM CONSTRUCTION

☑ **Plank fully**
- ○ Each platform on all working levels of scaffolds must be fully planked or decked with no more than a 1-inch space between the decking/platform units and the upright supports.
- ○ If there is not enough space to plank/deck fully, then you must plank/deck as much as you can.

- ○ All working platforms must be 18 inches wide for most scaffolds.

Exception: The decking/platforms for ladder jack, pump jack, top plate, trestle, and roof bracket scaffolds should be at least 12 inches wide.

- ○ If using the platform as a walkway, or for erecting or dismantling the scaffold, you only have to deck as much as necessary to ensure worker safety.
- ○ Wood scaffold planks should be nominal 2″ × 10″ (actual 1½″ × 9¼″) and must be Scaffold Grade Planks or equivalent. Which means that planks must bear the stamp of a grading agency approved by the American Lumber Standard Committee or equivalent. See appendix C for examples.

☑ **Erect scaffolds close to the face of the work**
- ○ The front edge of the platform must be within 14 inches of the face of the work for most operations. If this is not possible, workers must be protected with guardrails or personal fall arrest systems.

Capacidad

Cada andamio debe ser capaz de aguantar su propio peso y por lo menos 4 veces la carga prevista. La carga prevista incluye los trabajadores, el equipo, las herramientas y los materiales.

A menos que se indique lo contrario, esta sección corresponde a los andamios que suelen utilizarse en el ramo de la construcción residencial. Antes de montar un andamio, repase todas las secciones del reglamento para asegurarse de seguir los requisitos de la OSHA.

CONSTRUCCIÓN DE UN ANDAMIO DE PLATAFORMA

☑ **Cubrir completamente con tablones**

○ Cada plataforma de todos los niveles de trabajo en los andamios se debe cubrir completamente con tablones o entarimado sin exceder el espacio de 1 pulgada entre las tablas/unidades de plataforma y los soportes verticales.

○ Si no hay suficiente espacio para cubrirlo completamente con tablones/entarimado, se deberá cubrir la mayor parte posible.

○ Las plataformas sobre las que se trabajará deben tener un ancho de 18 pulgadas.

Excepción: Se debe contra con un ancho de por lo menos 12 pulgadas en el caso de tablones/plataformas para andamios de escalera, andamios de mecanismo de trinquete, andamios con ménsula para placa superior y para techo.

○ Si utilizará la plataforma como pasarela, o para montar o desmontar el andamio, sólo tiene que poner el entarimado necesario para que el trabajador no corra peligro.

○ Los tablones para andamio deben ser de 2″ × 10″ (nominal) 1½″ × 9¼″ (efectivo) y deben ser de calidad para andamio (*scaffold plank grade*) o su equivalente. Eso significa que los tablones deben tener el sello de un organismo calificador aprobado por el Comité Americano de Normas de la Madera (*American Lumber Standard Committee*) o su equivalente. En el apéndice C se proporcionan ejemplos.

☑ **Montar los andamios cerca del frente de trabajo**

○ En la mayoría de las obras, el borde delantero de la plataforma debe estar situado a no más de 14 pulgadas del frente de trabajo. Si eso no es posible, se deberá proteger a los trabajadores con barandales de seguridad o sistemas personales de protección contra caídas.

Exception: The distance between the edge of the platform and the face of the work can be 18 inches when plastering and lathing.

- ○ The maximum distance from the face for outrigger scaffolds is 3 inches. This is commonly used on fabricated frame scaffolds.

☑ **Secure and cleat the platform planking**

- ○ Platforms and planking must be cleated and/or attached to the scaffold or must extend at least 6 inches past the supports.
- ○ Platforms or planks **10 feet** in length *or less* cannot extend past the supports more than **12 inches** unless there is support for the cantilevered sections or guardrails that block employee access to the cantilevered end.

- ○ Platforms or planks *greater than* **10 feet** in length cannot extend past the supports more than **18 inches** unless there is support for the cantilevered sections or guardrails that block employee access to the cantilevered end.
- ○ If workers cannot access those cantilevered sections, no support for that section of the platform is needed.

☑ **Creating longer platform planking**

- ○ When creating longer platforms be sure that adjoining ends of the plank rest on separate supports or are secured.

- ○ Each end of planks must have 12 inches of overlap on the supports; otherwise, ends must be nailed or somehow secured together.

☑ **Keep the wood planks/platforms in good shape**

- ○ Tops and bottoms of work platforms must not be painted with anything that will hide defects.
- ○ They may be coated with wood preservatives, fire-retardant finishes, and slip-resistant finishes; how-

Excepción: La distancia entre el borde la plataforma y el frente de trabajo puede encontrarse a 18 pulgadas para enyesado y enlistonado.

○ La máxima distancia desde la cara exterior es de 3 pulgadas para andamios tipo volado. Comúnmente se usa en los andamios de marco fabricado.

☑ **Asegurar y sujetar los tablones con abrazaderas**

○ Las plataformas y tablones se deben sujetar con abrazaderas o afianzar al andamio o deben extenderse por lo menos 6 pulgadas más allá de los soportes.

○ Si algún tablón o plataforma tiene **10 pies** de longitud *o menos*, el vuelo no puede exceder los soportes en más de **12 pulgadas**, a menos que las secciones voladizas tengan soporte o barandales de seguridad para bloquear el acceso al extremo en voladizo por parte de los empleados.

○ El vuelo de las plataformas de *más de* **10 pies** de longitud no puede exceder los soportes en más de **18 pulgadas**, a menos que las secciones voladizas tengan soporte o barandales de seguridad para bloquear el acceso al extremo en voladizo por parte de los empleados.

○ Si los trabajadores no tienen acceso a esas secciones voladizas, no se requiere soporte para las mismas.

☑ **Crear tableado para plataformas largas**

○ Al crear plataformas más largas, es necesario verificar que los extremos de los tablones estén soportados cada uno en la junta en diferentes soportes o que estén afianzados.

○ Cada extremo de los tablones debe tener un traslape de 12 pulgadas sobre los soportes; de lo contrario, los extremos se deberán clavar o asegurar por algún otro medio.

☑ **Mantener los tablones/plataformas en buena condición**

○ No se debe pintar ninguna cara de las plataformas con productos que pudieran disimular defectos.

○ Se les puede aplicar algún conservante de madera, revestimientos ignífugos y acabados antirresbalantes; sin embargo, el acabado deberá ser transparente o

ever, the coating must be clear or translucent and may not obscure the top or bottom wood surfaces.

○ Only sides can be painted for identification.

Checking of Scaffold Boards

A board should not be used if:

☑ Either end is split so much as to cause a weakness.

☑ It is damaged by fracture or saw cut, is splintered, has nails sticking out of it, or has a lot of concrete or plaster sticking to it.

☑ It has had oil, corrosive liquid, or acid spilled on it.

☑ It has any part painted (which may cover up a weakness or/defect).

☑ It is excessively warped or any part is decayed.

☑ It has been overloaded or used for other purposes.

CRITERIA FOR SUPPORTED SCAFFOLDS

Most scaffolds used in the residential construction industry are supported scaffolds. Some basic rules must be followed to ensure that your scaffolds are properly supported.

● All scaffolds must be built and braced according to the manufacturer's specifications to prevent tipping. OSHA also requires that you follow some very specific requirements listed in the regulation.

● Supported scaffold feet, poles, legs, posts, frames, and uprights must bear on base plates and mud sills. They must rest on a firm, stable foundation.

● Do not use makeshift objects (blocks, brick, etc.) to support the scaffold feet.

● Do not use front-end loaders or similar equipment to support scaffolds unless they have been designed for that use by the manufacturer.

● Do not use forklifts to support scaffolds unless the entire platform is attached to the fork per manufacturer recommendations and the lift is not moved horizontally while workers are on the platform.

● Make sure all legs, uprights, posts, and frames are plumb and fully braced to prevent swaying.

translúcido y no debe oscurecer ni la cara anterior ni la posterior de la madera.

○ Solamente los costados se pueden pintar con fines de identificación.

Revisar las Tablas del Andamio

No se deberá usar ninguna tabla:

☑ Que tenga fisuras en los extremos, que pudieran provocar debilidad.

☑ Qué esté dañada por fractura o corte de sierra, que esté astillada, que tenga clavos salidos o que tenga pegado mucho concreto o yeso.

☑ Sobre la que se haya derramado aceite, líquido corrosivo o ácido.

☑ Que tenga pintada alguna parte (que pudiera disimular una debilidad o defecto).

☑ Que esté excesivamente pandeada o que tenga a alguna parte podrida.

☑ Sobre la que se haya puesto demasiado peso o que haya sido utilizada para otros fines.

CRITERIOS PARA LOS ANDAMIOS CON SOPORTE

En su mayoría los andamios que se utilizan en la construcción residencial son del tipo soportado. Se deben observar ciertas reglas básicas para asegurar que los andamios tengan los soportes apropiados.

● Todos los andamios se deberán armar y arriostrar de conformidad con las especificaciones del fabricante para evitar que se vuelquen. OSHA también dispone que hay que seguir ciertos requisitos muy específicos enumerados en la norma.

● Las patas, postes, sostenes, puntales, estructuras y montantes deben apoyarse sobre placas de base y los durmientes (soleras). Deben asentarse sobre un cimiento firme y estable.

● No se deben utilizar objetos pequeños (tabiques, ladrillos, etc.) para soportar las patas de los andamio.

● No se deben utilizar cargadores de ataque frontal a menos que hayan sido designadas para ese uso por el fabricante.

● No se deben utilizar elevadores de horquilla para soportar los andamios a menos que toda la plataforma esté fijada a la horquilla de conformidad con las recomendaciones del fabricante y no se mueva el elevador de horquilla en sentido horizontal cuando los trabajadores estén en la plataforma.

● Verifique que todos los sostenes, montantes, puntales y estructuras están a plomo y totalmente fijos para prevenir los vaivenes.

Access

Access onto scaffolds is an important part of scaffold safety. Scaffold platforms more than 2 feet above or below the access point must have portable, hook-on, or attachable ladders or scaffold stairways to allow workers to get on and off the scaffold.

You can have direct access from another scaffold or the structure as long as it is not more than 14 inches away horizontally and not more than 24 inches vertically.

NOTE: Cross braces can't be used to climb on or off scaffolds.

Ladders used for access must be positioned and secured to prevent the scaffold from tipping, and the bottom rung cannot be more than 24 inches above the ground or floor.

Make sure your hook-on or attachable ladders are specifically designed for use with the type of scaffold used. Rungs must be at least 11½ inches long and have a maximum uniform spacing of 16¾ inches between the rungs.

Acceso

El acceso a los andamios es parte importante de su seguridad. Las plataformas de andamio que se encuentren a más de 2 pies por encima o por debajo del punto de acceso deberán tener escaleras enganchables y portátiles o escaleras de andamio para que los trabajadores se puedan subir y bajar del andamio.

El acceso puede ser desde otro andamio o la estructura misma, siempre y cuando no esté a más de 14 pulgadas horizontalmente y no más de 24 pulgadas verticalmente.

NOTA: Las riostras no se pueden usar para subirse o bajarse de los andamios.

Las escaleras utilizadas para acceso se deben situar y afianzar para impedir que el andamio se vuelque y el travesaño inferior no puede estar a más de 24 pulgadas del suelo o piso.

Es necesario verificar que la escalera de gancho o escalera atable haya sido diseñada específicamente para usar con el tipo de andamio en cuestión. Los travesaños debe tener una longitud mínima de 11½ pulgadas y una distancia de separación uniforme de 16¾ entre cada uno.

Use

Scaffolds must be used properly to ensure worker safety and must not be loaded in excess of their design load or rated capacities.

The competent person must inspect the scaffold and its parts before each workshift and after any event that may weaken the scaffold. Listed below are some of the actions to avoid when using scaffolds.

- **Do not** use damaged parts that affect the strength of the scaffold.
- **Do not** move a scaffold while workers are on it, unless it is a mobile scaffold and designed to be moved when workers are on the scaffold.
- **Do not** swing loads near or on scaffolds unless you use a tag line.
- **Do not** work on scaffolds in bad weather or high winds unless the competent person decided that it is safe to do so.
- **Do not** allow workers to get on scaffolds that contain snow, ice, or other slippery material except as necessary for removal of such materials.
- **Do not** let extra material build up on the platforms.

- **Do not** let wood planks deflect more than 1/60 of the span, that is 2 inches for a 10 foot plank.
- **Do not** use ladders, boxes, barrels or other makeshift contraptions to raise worker heights.
- **Do not** erect, use, alter, or move scaffolds within 10 feet of overhead high voltage power lines.

Uso

Los andamios se deben usar de la manera correcta para garantizar la seguridad de los trabajadores y no se deben cargar más allá de su carga máxima prevista o su capacidad nominal.

La persona competente debe inspeccionar el andamio y sus componentes antes de cada turno de trabajo y después de todo acontecimiento que pudiera debilitar el andamio. A continuación se enumeran algunas de las acciones que se deben evitar al usar andamios.

● No usar piezas dañadas que pudieran afectar la resistencia del andamio.

● No mover un andamio con trabajadores encima a menos que se trate de un andamio móvil diseñado para ser trasladado cuando los trabajadores se encuentran sobre él.

● No izar cargas cerca o sobre los andamios a menos que se utilice un cabo de seguridad.

● No trabajar sobre andamios en tiempo malo ni con vientos fuertes a menos que la persona competente haya decidido que se puede hacer sin peligro.

● No permitir que los trabajadores se suban a andamios que tengan nieve, hielo o cualquier otro material resbaloso, salvo en la medida necesaria para quitar dichos materiales.

● No permitir que se acumule ninguna clase de material sobre las plataformas.

● No permitir que los tablones se aparten más de 1/60 del vuelo, es decir 2 pulgadas en el caso de un tablón de 10 pies.

● No utilizar escaleras, cajas, barriles ni ningún otro aparato improvisado para elevar la altura del trabajador.

● No armar, usar, alterar ni trasladar andamios a menos de 10 pies de donde haya cables eléctricos aéreos.

The clearance between scaffolds and power lines must be as follows:

Insulated Lines Voltage	Minimum Distance	Alternatives
Less than 300 volts	3 feet	NA
300 volts to 50 kv	10 feet	NA
More than 50 kv	10 feet plus 0.4 inches for each 1 kv over 50 kv	2 times the length of the line insulator, but never less than 10 feet
Uninsulated Lines Voltage	**Minimum Distance**	**Alternatives**
Less than 50 kv	10 feet	NA
More than 50 kv	10 feet plus 0.4 inches for each 1 kv over 50 kv	2 times the length of the line insulator, but never less than 10 feet

REQUISITOS GENERALES **19**

El margen de seguridad entre los andamios y los cables eléctricos debe ser como sigue:

Cables aislados Tensión	Distancia mínima	Alternativas
Menos de 300 voltios	3 pies	No corresponde
300 voltios a 50 kv	10 pies	No corresponde
Más de 50 kv	10 pies más 0.4 pulgadas por cada 1 kv sobre 50 kv	2 veces el largo del aislador del cable, pero nunca menos de 10 pies
Cables no aislados **Tensión**	**Distancia mínima**	**Alternativas**
Menos de 50 kv	10 pies	No corresponde
Más de 50 kv	10 pies más 0.4 pulgadas por cada 1 kv sobre 50 kv	2 veces el largo del aislador del cable, pero nunca menos de 10 pies

Fall Protection

Fall protection must be provided on all scaffolds greater than 10 feet high. (In California protection must be provided on all scaffolds greater than 7 feet high.) Usually this is done with guardrails. Guardrail systems must be installed before the scaffold is released for use by employees other than during the erection and dismantling of scaffold. Install guardrails along all open sides and ends, and you must comply with the following requirements:

☑ Toprails must be installed between 39 and 45 inches high.
☑ Midrails must be installed halfway between the platform and the toprail. If using mesh or panels, install them from the top to bottom of the guardrail.

☑ Toprails must withstand 200 pounds of downward or outward force, and must not be made of steel or plastic banding. Rail ends must not hang over the edge of scaffolds.
☑ All midrails must withstand at least 150 pounds of downward or outward force.

Cross bracing can be used in place of toprails or midrails (but not both at the same time) if the cross is between 20 and 30 inches above the platform for the midrail, or 38 to 48 inches above the platform for the toprail, and the endpoints are not more than 48 inches apart.

Guardrails must be surfaced to prevent puncture wounds or lacerations on workers and to prevent clothing from getting caught.

When using ladder jack scaffolds, a personal fall arrest system must be used when the scaffold height is greater than 10 feet.

On crawling boards/chicken ladders, a personal fall arrest system, or a grab rope alongside the crawling board must be used to protect workers.

Protección Contra Caídas

Se debe proporcionar protección contra caídas en todos los andamios de más de 10 pies de altura. En California es necesario tener protección en andamios con una altura en exceso de 7 pies Dicha protección suele ser en forma de barandales de seguridad. Los sistemas de barandales se deben instalar antes de que se permita a los empleados utilizar el andamio, salvo para fines de montaje y desmontaje del mismo. Los barandales de seguridad se deben instalar a lo largo de todos los lados abiertos y se deberán cumplir los siguientes requisitos:

- ☑ Instalar barandales superiores a una altura de 39 y 45 pulgadas.
- ☑ Instalar travesaños intermedios justo entre la plataforma y el barandal superior. Si se utiliza malla o paneles, se deben instalar desde la parte superior hacia la parte inferior del barandal de seguridad.
- ☑ Los barandales superiores deben ser capaces de aguantar 200 libras de fuerza hacia abajo o hacia fuera y no deben estar hechos de bandas de acero ni de plástico. Los extremos de los barandales no deben sobrepasar la orilla del andamio.
- ☑ Todos los travesaños intermedios deben ser capaces de soportar 150 libras de fuerza hacia abajo o hacia afuera.

Se pueden usar riostras en lugar de barandales superiores y travesaños intermedios (pero no ambos al mismo tiempo) si el cruce se encuentra entre 20 y 30 pulgadas por encima de la plataforma, en caso del travesaño intermedio, o 38 a 48 pulgadas por encima de la plataforma en el caso del barandal superior y los extremos no tienen una separación mayor a 48 pulgadas.

Los barandales de seguridad deben tener una superficie apropiada para prevenir las lesiones por punción y las laceraciones y para evitar que la ropa se enganche.

Cuando se utilice un andamio de escalera de más de 10 pies de altura, se deberá utilizar un sistema personal de protección contra caídas.

En los tablones con listones o escaleras rampantes se deberá utilizar un sistema personal de protección contra caídas o un cabo de retención para proteger a los trabajadores.

Falling Object Protection

Falling off scaffolds isn't the only threat to worker safety. Often tools and materials are knocked over or fall off the scaffold and hit workers.

Anyone working on or around a scaffold must wear a hard hat.

Workers on or below scaffolds must be protected from falling objects. This can be done with barricades, toeboards, mesh, screens, or equivalent measures. Securing large or heavy objects and materials away from the edge can protect workers.

Toeboards must be placed as high as the materials that can fall off the scaffold. They must be at least 3½ inches high and must be able to withstand 50 pounds of force.

Protección Contra Objetos en Caída

Caerse de un andamio no es el único peligro que corre el trabajador. A menudo se caen herramientas o materiales del andamio que golpean a los trabajadores.

Cualquier persona que trabaje en o alrededor de un andamio debe usar casco.

Los trabajadores que se encuentran sobre los andamios o debajo de ellos deben estar protegidos contra objetos en caída. Eso se puede hacer con barricadas, guardapiés, malla, cercas o medios similares. Afianzar los objetos grandes o pesados alejados de la orilla puede proteger a los trabajadores.

Los guardapiés (tablas de guarda) se deben colocar a la altura del material que se podría caer del andamio. Deben tener una altura mínima de 3½ pulgadas y deben ser capaces de aguantar 50 libras de fuerza.

Types of Scaffold

Fabricated Frame Scaffold
Pump Jack Scaffold
Ladder Jack Scaffold
Saw Horse Scaffold
Step, Platform, or Trestle Ladder Scaffold
Mobile Scaffolds
Mobile Utility Scaffold
Roof Bracket Scaffold
Carpenters' Wall Bracket Scaffold
Carpenters' Top Plate Bracket Scaffold
Aerial Lifts

Tipos de Andamio

Andamios Hechos Con Tubos De Acero
Andamios de Mecanismo de Trinquete
Andamios de Mecanismo de Trinquete
Andamios de Caballete de Aserrar
Andamios de Escalón, Plataforma y Caballete
Andamio Móvil
Andamio Móvil para Servicio General
Andamio de Ménsula de Techo
Andamio de Carpintero Hecho con Ménsulas para Pared
Andamio de Carpintero Hecho con Ménsulas para la Placa
    Superior
Elevadores Aéreos

Fabricated Frame Scaffolds (tubular—welded frame scaffold)

In addition to following the manufacturer's recommendations, be sure you follow the rules listed below.

☑ All scaffolding must be inspected before use to insure that it is in good condition.

☑ Do not use scaffold if there are damaged parts such as rust.

Figure 1. This type of scaffold consists of a platform(s) supported on fabricated end frames.

Andamios Hechos con Tubos de Acero

Además de seguir las recomendaciones del fabricante, también es imprescindible seguir las reglas enumeradas a continuación.

- ☑ Todo andamio deberá ser inspeccionado antes de ser utilizado a fin de verificar que se encuentra en buen estado.
- ☑ No utilizar ningún andamio si tiene piezas dañadas o señales de oxidación.

Figura 1. Este tipo de andamio consiste en una o varias plataformas soportadas sobre bastidores o marcos en los extremos.

Figure 2. Prior to scaffold erection, ensure that the scaffold rests on a firm, stable foundation.

Figura 2. Antes de montar el andamio, verificar que la base sea firme y estable.

Figure 3. All scaffolds must have a proper base, including adjustable feet, base plates, a mud sill, and be level, and capable of supporting four times the maximum expected load.

Figura 3. Todos los andamios deben tener una base adecuada, nivelada, que incluye patas ajustables, placas de base, un durmiente o solera y que sea capaz de aguantar cuatro veces la carga máxima prevista.

Figure 4. Bricks and cement blocks cannot be used for support.

Figure 5. Level the scaffold at the bearers and side posts.

Figura 4. Los ladrillos y tabiques de concreto no se pueden usar como soportes.

Figura 5. Nivelar el andamio en los soportes y los puntales laterales.

Figure 6. Plumb/level and square all scaffolds.

Figure 7. Vertical members of frames must be secured laterally. Secure cross bracing so that the frame is squared and aligned.

Figura 6. Aplomar/nivelar y escuadrar todos los andamios.

Figura 7. Los miembros verticales de la estructura se deben afianzar lateralmente. Verificar que la estructura esté en escuadra y alineada al afianzar las riostras.

When moving scaffold planks to the next level, the existing platform should not be removed until the new end frames are set in place and braced.

Figure 8. Scaffolds must be fully planked at the working level and have a safe means of access. The attached ladder allows workers to get on and off the scaffold safely.

Al desplazar las tablas de andamio al siguiente nivel, no se deberá quitar la plataforma existente sino hasta que los nuevos marcos de los extremos estén colocados y fijados con riostras.

Figura 8. La plataforma de los andamios debe estar completamente ocupada con tablas en el nivel de trabajo y debe tener un medio de acceso seguro. La escalera fija le permite al trabajador subir y bajar del andamio sin peligro.

Figure 9. Climbing scaffold members and braces is not an acceptable means of access.

Figure 10. Plank boards must be scaffold grade, or equivalent. Solid sawn and laminated plank must be a minimum of 2 inches by 10 inches nominal in size, or equivalent.

Figure 11. A plank that is 10 feet in length or less must extend at least 6 inches, or must be cleated or attached to the scaffold frame.

Figura 9. Treparse por el andamio no es una manera aceptable de obtener acceso.

Figura 10. Los tablones de la plataforma deben ser de calidad para andamios o su equivalente. Los tablones de madera sólida ya serruchados y los de madera laminada deben ser de 2 pulgadas por 10 pulgadas (nominal) o su equivalente.

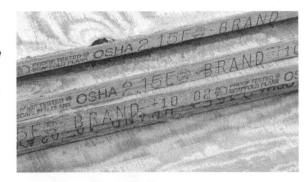

Figura 11. Un tablón que no sobre pase 10 pies de longitud debe tener un vuelo de por lo menos 6 pulgadas, o se deberá asegurar con abrazaderas o de alguna manera fijarse al marco del andamio.

Figure 12. A toe board must be erected along the edge of the platform. The boards must be al least 3½ inches high or as high as the material on the scaffold to prevent objects from falling off.

Figure 13. Properly installed guardrails must be used on scaffolds more than 10 feet above the ground or floor surface. (7 feet in California.)

Figura 12. Se debe colocar un guardapiés a lo largo del borde la plataforma. Para evitar que los objetos se caigan, las tablas deben tener una altura mínima de 3½ pulgadas o la misma altura que el material que está en el andamio.

Figura 13. Se debe usar barandales correctamente instalados en todos los andamios de más de 10 pies de altura sobre el suelo o la superficie del piso. (7 pies en California.)

Figure 14. Properly installed guardrails must be used on scaffolds more than 10 feet above the ground or floor surface. (7 feet in California.)

Figure 15. Frames and panels must be joined by couplings, stacking pins, or other means to keep the frame secure and to prevent frame uplift.

Figura 14. Se debe usar barandales correctamente instalados en todos los andamios de más de 10 pies de altura sobre el suelo o la superficie del piso. (7 pies en California.)

Figura 15. Los marcos y paneles se deben unir con acoplamientos, pernos u otros medios para que el marco quede seguro y no se levante.

Pump Jack Scaffolds

A pump jack scaffold is a supported scaffold consisting of a platform supported by vertical poles and movable brackets.

Vertical pole members can be constructed of wood or manufactured aluminum poles.

Aluminum Pole Pump Jack Scaffolds are more stable, offer excellent strength, and can prove to be cheaper to maintain in the long run.

When using pump jack scaffolds, builders often have the actual pump jack unit but do not have the other required elements of a properly built pump jack scaffold, such as guardrails or tie-ins. A review of the following information should remind you how to build a pump jack scaffold safely.

☑ Brackets, braces, and accessories must be made from metal plates and angles.
☑ Each bracket must have two gripping mechanisms to prevent slippage.

When using wood poles with pump jacks they must be straight-grained; free of shakes; free of large, loose, or dead knots; and without other defects that could weaken the pole. Wood poles that are built of two continuous lengths must be joined together with the seam parallel.

When 2 × 4s are spliced together to make a pole, mending plates must be used to maintain the full strength of the lumber.

NOTE: Wood poles should not exceed 30 feet.

Andamios de Mecanismo de Trinquete

El andamio de mecanismo de trinquete es un andamio con soporte que consiste en plataformas que se apoyan sobre postes verticales y ménsulas móviles.

Los miembros verticales de poste pueden construirse de madera o de postes fabricados de aluminio.

Los andamios de mecanismo de trinquete hechos de postes de aluminio son más estables, ofrecen una resistencia excelente y pueden resultar más económicos a largo plazo en cuanto a su mantenimiento.

Cuando utilizan andamios de mecanismo de trinquete, a menudo los contratistas tienen la unidad básica sin los demás elementos requeridos para un andamio de mecanismo de trinquete correctamente armado, tales como los barandales de seguridad y conectores. La siguiente información explica cómo construir un andamio de mecanismo de trinquete que sea seguro.

☑ Las ménsulas, riostras y accesorios deben estar hechos de placas de metal y angulares.

☑ Cada ménsula debe tener dos mecanismos de sujeción para impedir que se resbale.

Cuando se utilizan postes de madera con andamios de mecanismo de trinquete, los postes deben tener el hilo recto; no deben tener ripias, no deben tener nudos grandes, sueltos o muertos; y no deben tener ningún otro defecto que pudiera debilitar el poste. Los postes de madera construidos a partir de dos largos continuos se deben unir con la unión paralela.

Cuando se ensamblan tablas de 2×4 para formar un poste, se deberán utilizar placas de reparación para conservar toda la resistencia de la madera.

NOTA: Los postes de madera no deben exceder 30 pies de largo.

Figure 16. Pump jack scaffolds are one of the most common scaffolds used in the residential construction industry. Usually, they are used during siding when work locations change a lot and are considered light duty scaffolding.

Figura 16. Los andamios de mecanismo de trinquete son uno de los tipos de andamio más comunes que se utilizan en la industria de la construcción residencial. Por lo general se usan durante la instalación del revestimiento exterior, cuando el lugar de trabajo cambia mucho y se considera andamio de uso ligero.

Figure 17. A worker preparing to adjust an aluminum pole pump jack scaffold prior to work, with properly installed end guardrails.

NOTE: The work bench where the materials are stored may be used as a guardrail if it fits the proper height. Standing on the workbench is prohibited.

Figura 17. Un trabajador se prepara para ajustar el andamio antes de trabajar; tiene barandales de seguridad correctamente instalados.

NOTA: El banco de trabajo donde se guardan los materiales se puede usar como barandal de seguridad siempre que sea de la altura correcta. Se prohíbe pararse sobre el banco de trabajo.

Figure 18. When using pump jack scaffolds, builders often have the actual pump jack unit but do not have the other required elements of a properly built pump jack scaffold, such as guardrails or tie-ins.

Figura 18. Cuando utilizan andamios de mecanismo de trinquete, a menudo los contratistas tienen la unidad básica sin los demás elementos requeridos para un andamio de mecanismo de trinquete correctamente armado, tales como los barandales de seguridad y conectores.

Figure 19. Poles must be attached to the structure with rigid triangle braces or tie-ins at the top, bottom, and any other locations necessary to keep the scaffold secure.

Figura 19. Los postes se deben fijar a la estructura con riostras triangulares rígidas o conectores para que el andamio quede seguro en la parte superior, inferior y cualquier otro lugar necesario.

Figure 20. Triangle brace installed at roof.

Figura 20. Riostra triangular instalada en el techo.

Figure 21a. Two examples of the correct use of mud sills.

Figure 21b.

*Figura 21a. Dos ejemplos
del uso correcto de soleras.*

Figura 21b.

Figure 22. All guardrails must be installed, this includes end rails.

Figura 22. Se deben instalar todos los barandales de seguridad, incluidos los de los extremos.

Figure 23. Two workers are installing a guardrail system prior to use.

*Figura 23. Dos trabajadores
están instalando un sistema
de barandales de seguridad
antes de usar el andamio.*

Ladder Jack Scaffolds

☑ Ladder jack scaffolds must not exceed 20 feet in height or be bridged together.

☑ Job-built ladders are not allowed to be used to support the scaffold. Ladders must be properly manufactured and sturdy.

☑ The ladder jack must be assembled so that the weight bears on the side rails and ladder rungs. The bearing must be at least 10 inches in length on each rung.

☑ Ladders used to support ladder jacks must be equipped with devices to prevent slipping.

NOTE: Remember, when work is being done higher than 10 feet on a ladder jack, workers must use a personal fall arrest system to prevent falls.

Figure 24. A ladder jack scaffold is a supported scaffold consisting of a platform resting on brackets attached to two ladders.

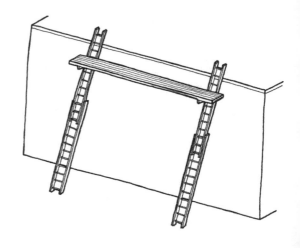

Andamios de Escalera

☑ Los andamios de escalera no deben exceder 20 pies de altura ni se deben unir mediante puentes.

☑ No se permite utilizar escaleras construidas en la obra para soportar el andamio. Las escaleras deben ser escaleras fabricadas correctamente y resistentes.

☑ El andamio de escalera se debe montar de tal forma que el peso descanse sobre los rieles laterales y los travesaños. El punto de apoyo debe tener una longitud mínima de 10 pulgadas en cada travesaño.

☑ Las escaleras utilizadas para soportar andamios de escalera deben estar equipadas con dispositivos para evitar que se resbalen.

NOTA: Recuerde que cuando se trabaja a una altura de más de 10 pies en un andamio de escalera los trabajadores deben utilizar un sistema personal de protección contra caídas para prevenir las mismas.

Figura 24. El andamio de escalera es un andamio soportado que consiste en una plataforma que descansa sobre ménsulas fijadas a dos escaleras.

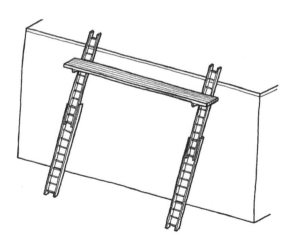

Figure 25. Ladder jack scaffolds are used when installing siding on a structure and other short term projects.

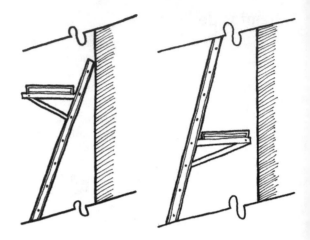

Figura 25. Los andamios de escalera se usan para la instalación del revestimiento exterior de una estructura y otros proyectos de corto plazo.

Figure 26. The worker is wearing a full body harness attached to a lanyard. The rope grab is attached to a lifeline connected to an approved 5000 pound rated anchor connected to the roof.

Figura 26. El trabajador está usando un arnés (arreos) de cuerpo completo amarrado a un cabo acollador. La soga de agarre está amarrada a un cabo salvavidas conectado a un anclaje aprobado de aguante nominal de 5000 libras, atado al techo.

Figure 27. The worker is adjusting the position of his lanyard which will allow him to reach his work.

Figura 27. El trabajador está ajustando la posición de su cabo acollador, lo cual le permitirá alcanzar su trabajo.

Figure 28. Personal fall arrest system (PFAS) is a system used to stop an employee's fall. It consists of an anchorage, connectors, a body harness and may include a lanyard, deceleration device, lifeline, or combination of these.

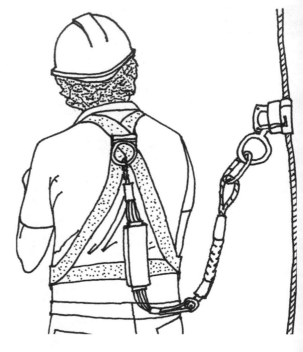

Figura 28. El sistema personal de protección contra caídas (SPPCC) es un sistema que se usa para detener la caída de un trabajador. Consiste en un anclaje, conectores, arnés y puede incluir acollador, dispositivo de desaceleración, cabo salvavidas o cualquier combinación de ellos.

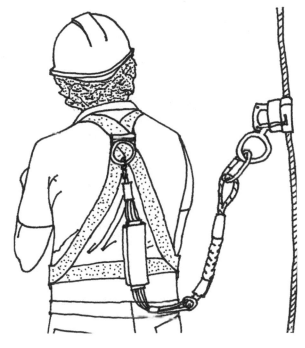

Saw Horse Scaffolds

Generally, horse scaffolds are used during truss erection and raftering procedures to keep workers from getting on the top plate.

Saw horse scaffolds cannot have more than 2 levels or be over 10 feet.

☑ The second level has to be placed right on top of the first and must be crossed braced with the legs nailed down or secured to prevent the scaffold from moving.

☑ Platforms cannot be placed higher than the next-to-last rung or step. Scaffolds cannot be bridged together.

☑ All ladders used with step, platform, or trestle ladder scaffolds must be manufactured properly and support the scaffold.

☑ Job-built ladders cannot be used to support scaffolds.

☑ Ladders used to support step, platform, and trestle scaffolds have to be equipped with devices to prevent slipping.

Andamios de Caballete de Aserrar

En general, los andamios de caballete se usan durante el montaje de las armaduras de y los trabajos con cabrios para que los trabajadores no se pongan en la placa superior.

Los andamios de caballete de aserrar no pueden tener más de 2 niveles ni más de 10 pies de altura.

☑ El segundo nivel debe estar colocado directamente sobre el primero y debe tener arriostramiento en cruz con las patas clavadas o aseguradas para impedir que el andamio se mueva.

☑ Las plataformas no se pueden colocar más alto que el penúltimo travesaño o escalón. No se pueden unir dos andamios.

☑ Todas las escaleras utilizadas con andamios de escalón, plataforma o escalera de caballete deben estar fabricadas correctamente y deben soportar el andamio.

☑ No se pueden usar escaleras construidas en la obra para apoyar los andamios.

☑ Las escaleras utilizadas para apoyar los andamios de escalón, plataforma y caballete tienen que estar equipadas con dispositivos para evitar que se resbalen.

Figure 29. A saw horse scaffold is a supported scaffold consisting of a platform (must be scaffold grade planking) supported by construction horses (saw horses).

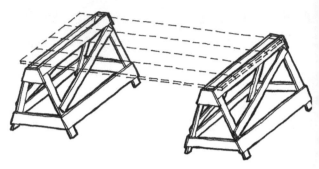

Figura 29. Un andamio de caballete de aserrar es un andamio soportado que consiste en una plataforma (debe ser de calidad andamio) soportada por caballetes de construcción.

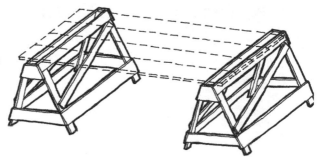

Step, Platform, and Trestle Ladder Scaffolds

Figure 30. A step, platform, or trestle ladder scaffold is a platform (scaffold grade planking) resting directly on the rungs of step ladders or trestle ladders.

Andamios de Escalón, Plataforma y Caballete

Figura 30. Un andamio de escalón, plataforma o caballete es una plataforma (con tablas de calidad para andamio) que descansa directamente sobre los travesaños de escaleras de mano o de caballete.

Figure 31. This worker is not required to have a personal fall arrest system (PFAS) when working at 10 feet or below.

Figura 31. Este trabajador no tiene que tener un sistema personal de protección contra caídas (SPPCC) cuando trabaja a una altura de 10 pies o menos.

Mobile Scaffold

A mobile scaffold is a powered or unpowered, portable, caster or wheel-mounted supported scaffold.

Figure 32. Cross, horizontal, and diagonal braces must be secured to prevent collapse. Mobile scaffolds must have the vertical members secured laterally so that the scaffold is automatically plumb and aligned.

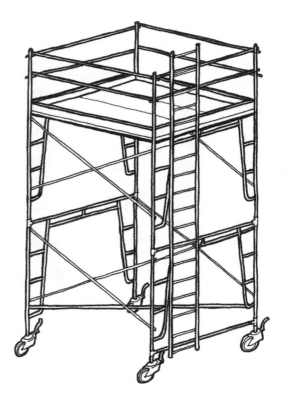

Andamio Móvil

Un andamio móvil es un andamio soportado, con o sin motor, portátil con ruedas.

Figura 32. Las riostras cruzadas, horizontales y diagonales deben estar aseguradas para impedir el derrumbamiento. Los andamios móviles deben tener los miembros verticales asegurados lateralmente para que el andamio quede automáticamente aplomado y alineado.

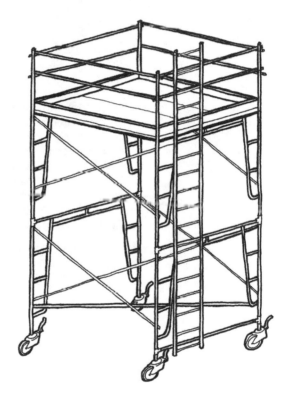

Figure 33. Caster wheels must be locked to prevent movement of the scaffold when it is stationary and the caster stems and wheels must be secured in place.

Platforms and planks must not extend beyond the supports unless stability is maintained.

When moving the scaffold, the base should be pushed on or near the bottom of the scaffold. During movement, mobile scaffolds must be stabilized to prevent tipping.

Scaffolds should not be moved while employees are on them, unless they have been designed by a registered professional engineer specifically for such movement and the following safe work practices are followed:

☑ The angle of the floor must be within 3 degrees of level.
☑ The height-to-width base ratio must be 2:1.
☑ Workers cannot be outside the end supports.

☑ Workers must be told the scaffold is moving prior to the move.
☑ Make sure there are no pits, holes, or obstructions on the floor.

Figura 33. Se les debe poner el seguro a las ruedas (roldanas) para que no se mueva el andamio cuando está estacionario.

El vuelo de las plataformas y tablas no debe exceder los soportes a menos que se mantenga la estabilidad.

Para mover el andamio se debe empujar la base en o cerca de la parte inferior del andamio. Los andamios móviles se deben estabilizar al moverlos para impedir que se vuelquen.

No se debe mover un andamio mientras estén encima los trabajadores, a menos que haya sido designado por un ingeniero profesional específicamente para dicho movimiento y se sigan estas prácticas de trabajo seguro:

- ☑ La inclinación del piso no debe sobrepasar 3 grados.
- ☑ La relación altura-anchura de la base debe ser 2:1.
- ☑ No puede haber trabajadores fuera de los soportes de los extremos.
- ☑ Se les tiene que avisar a los trabajadores que van a mover el andamio antes de hacerlo.
- ☑ Es necesario verificar que no haya fosos, hoyos ni obstrucciones en el piso.

Figure 34. Mobile scaffold properly erected with safe access by manufacture's built-in ladder system. All wheels are locked.

Figura 34. Andamio móvil montado correctamente con acceso seguro en el sistema de escalera incorporado del fabricante. Todas las ruedas tienen puesto el seguro.

Figure 35. Guardrails are installed on all sides of this mobile scaffold.

Figura 35. Barandales de seguridad instalados en todos los lados del andamio móvil.

Figure 36. This working deck is fully planked using manufactured planks with hooks that secure over structural members. A chain for closing ladder access way is secured as midrail fall protection.

Figura 36. Este entarimado de trabajo se construyó en su totalidad con tablones manufacturados con ganchos que se cuelgan sobre los miembros estructurales. La cadena para cerrar el acceso a la escalera también sirve como travesaño intermedio de protección contra caídas.

Mobile Utility Scaffolds

A mobile utility scaffold is a small compact scaffolding unit designed primarily for interior use.

Mobile utility scaffolds have a lower maximum load rating as compared to fabricated frame mobile scaffolds.

Figure 37. This mobile utility scaffold allows the user to safely reach work areas whereas ladders or larger scaffolds are not feasible. Casters are locked and guardrails are installed.

Andamio Móvil para Servicio General

Un andamio móvil para servicio general es un andamio pequeño y compacto diseñado principalmente para el uso en interiores.

Los andamios móviles para servicio general tienen una menor capacidad máxima de carga en comparación con los andamios fabricados de tubos.

Figura 37. Este andamio móvil para servicio general le permite al usuario alcanzar sin peligro áreas de trabajo en las cuales no se puede usar una escalera o un andamio más grande. Las ruedas tienen puesto el seguro y los barandales están instalados.

Figure 38. This scaffold is ideally suited to dual-level surfaces and narrow work areas as illustrated.

Figura 38. Este andamio es ideal para superficies de dos niveles y lugares de trabajo angostos, como se muestra en la ilustración.

Roof Bracket Scaffolds

A roof bracket scaffold is a rooftop supported scaffold consisting of a platform resting on angular-shaped supports.

If you are using roof bracket scaffold, the scaffold plank must be level.

Platforms for roof brackets can not be less than 12 inches.

Brackets must be secured to the roof; nailing them is usually most effective.

Figure 39. Worker performing roof work on roof bracket scaffold. Worker (out of the picture) is wearing a full body harness and grab lifeline lanyard connected to an approved attachment point rated for 5000 pounds.

Andamio de Ménsula de Techo

Un andamio de ménsula de techo es un andamio de techo soportado que consiste en una plataforma que descansa sobre soportes de forma angular.

Si está utilizando andamios de ménsula de techo, la tablazón debe estar nivelada.

Las plataformas para ménsulas de techo no pueden ser de menos de 12 pulgadas.

Las ménsulas deberán estar fijadas al techo; generalmente lo más eficaz es hacerlo con clavos.

Figura 39. Un trabajador hace trabajo de techo en un andamio con ménsulas para techo. El trabajador (no se muestra en la foto) tiene puesto un arnés de cuerpo entero y un cabo salvavidas conectado a un punto de anclaje aprobado con una resistencia nominal de 5000 libras.

Carpenters' Wall Bracket Scaffold

A carpenters' wall bracket scaffold is a supported scaffold consisting of a platform supported by brackets attached with bolts to building or structural walls.

Figure 40. Carpenters' wall bracket scaffolds that are built over 10 feet in height from the ground must include guardrails, mid-rails and toe boards on all open sides. In the alternative, the area below the scaffold where objects can fall must be barricaded and employees are not allowed to enter this hazardous area.

Andamio de Carpintero Hecho con Ménsulas para Pared

El andamio de carpintero hecho con ménsulas para pared es un andamio soportado que consiste en una plataforma soportada por ménsulas fijadas con pernos al edificio o las paredes estructurales.

Figura 40. Los andamios de carpintero hechos con ménsulas para pared y construidos a una altura de más de 10 pies del suelo deben incluir barandales de seguridad, travesaños intermedios y guardapiés en todos los lados abiertos. En la alternativa, el área que se encuentra debajo del andamio, hasta donde pueden caerse los objetos, debe estar cerrada con barricadas porque no se permite a los empleados entrar en esa zona peligrosa.

Figure 41. These end guard chains provide fall protection at the edges of this wall bracket scaffold.

Figura 41. Estas cadenas de protección en los extremos protegen contra caídas a lo largo de las orillas de este andamio hecho con ménsulas para pared.

Top Plate Scaffold

A top plate bracket scaffold is a scaffold supported by brackets that hook over or are attached (depends on manufacturer) to the top of a wall. This type of scaffold is similar to the carpenters' bracket scaffold and is used in residential construction for setting trusses, cutting tails, rolling floor joists on the second level. This scaffold type eliminates the need to build makeshift scaffolding that does not meet OSHA standards for scaffolding. This type of scaffold (and the wall) must be capable of supporting, without failure, its own weight and four times the intended load.

Figure 42. Properly erected Top Plate Scaffold. All guardrails are in place, which includes the end rails. Access can be gained through window or a secured ladder.

Andamio Hecho con Ménsulas
para la Placa Superior

Un andamio hecho con ménsulas para la placa superior es un andamio soportado por ménsulas que se cuelgan o se fijan (dependiendo del fabricante) a la parte superior de una pared. Este tipo de andamio es similar al andamio de carpintero hecho con ménsulas para pared y se utiliza en la construcción residencial para la instalación de armaduras, el corte de los extremos al mismo largo, la instalación de viguetas de piso en el segundo nivel. Con este tipo de andamio no es necesario construir andamios improvisados que no cumplan con los reglamentos de la OSHA para andamios. Este tipo de andamio (y la pared) debe ser capaz de soportar, sin falla, su propio peso y cuatro veces la carga prevista.

Figura 42. Andamio para placa superior correctamente ensamblado. Todos los barandales de protección están instalados, lo que incluye los barandales de los extremos. Se puede obtener acceso al andamio a través de una ventana o por medio de una escalera asegurada.

Figure 43. Framers can safely set roof trusses on second and third level of a structure.

Figure 44. Top plate scaffolds are re-usable and quick to install. They reduce the risk of injury by eliminating the need for workers to walk the top plate of walls.

Figura 43. Los carpinteros pueden instalar las armaduras de cubierta sin peligro en el segundo y tercer nivel de una estructura.

Figura 44. Los andamios para placa superior se pueden reutilizar y se instalan con facilidad. Reducen el riesgo de lesión pues se elimina la necesidad de que el trabajador camine sobre la placa superior de las paredes.

Figure 45. Workers can safely work within the structure eliminating the need for multiple ladders sets.

Figura 45. El trabajador puede trabajar sin peligro dentro de la estructura, lo cual elimina la necesidad de usar muchas escaleras.

Aerial Lifts

Aerial lifts are considered elevated work platforms so they fall under OSHA's Subpart L Scaffold Standard.

As jobsites become more automated, many builders will use aerial lifts or other types of mobile scaffolds for some framing activities and exterior finish work as well as for materials handling.

If you are going to use aerial lifts you need to ensure your employees know how to operate the equipment safely.

☑ Only use equipment approved for lifting personnel to do aerial work and operate lift in accordance with manufacturer's instructions. Forklifts, loaders, and other equipment designed for moving materials must not be used as elevated work platforms or to transport workers to elevated locations unless they have been specifically designed by the manufacturer for such use.

☑ Only use aerial lifts if you are trained and authorized to do so.

Figure 46. Wear a personal fall arrest system (PFAS) at all times when working from an aerial lift.

Elevadores Aéreos

Los elevadores aéreos se consideran plataformas de trabajo elevadas y por eso están abarcadas por la Norma de Andamios de OSHA (Subpart L Scaffold Standard).

A medida que las obras se vuelven cada vez más automatizadas, muchos constructores utilizarán elevadores aéreos y otras clases de andamios móviles para algunas actividades de ensamblado, trabajo de acabado de exteriores y para el manejo de materiales.

Si usted va a usar elevadores aéreos, será necesario que se asegure de que sus empleados sepan como operar el equipo sin peligro.

☑ Utilice únicamente equipo aprobado para izar personal para hacer trabajo aéreo y opere el elevador como se indica en las instrucciones del fabricante. Las horquillas, cargadoras y otras clases de equipo diseñado para mover materiales no se deben usar como plataformas de trabajo elevadas ni para transportar a los trabajadores a lugares elevados a menos que hayan sido diseñadas específicamente por el fabricante para ese fin.

☑ Utilice los elevadores aéreos únicamente si está adiestrado y autorizado para hacerlo.

Figura 46. Use un sistema personal de protección contra caídas (PFAS) en todo momento que esté trabajando en un elevador aéreo.

*Figure 47. A full body fall protection harness must be worn and the lanyard attached to the correct anchor point on the bucket or boom. **Do not** attach the lanyard to another point such as the structure, nearby pole, or piece of equipment. All fall protection equipment must be inspected for damage and defects before each use.*

*Figura 47. Se deberá usar un arnés de protección (arreaos) contra caídas de cuerpo completo y el cabo deberá estar atado al punto de anclaje correcto de la cubeta o pluma. **No** ate el cabo a otro punto, como la estructura o un poste o máquina cercana. El equipo de protección contra caídas se deberá inspeccionar antes de cada uso por si estuviera dañado o presentara defectos.*

Figure 48. Always stand on the floor of the basket. ***Do not*** *sit or climb on the edge of the basket, lean over the guardrails, or climb out of the basket.* ***Do not*** *use ladders or other objects to increase reach. Ensure the aerial lift is operated on a level and firm surface.*

Figure 49. ***Do not*** *move an occupied aerial lift with the boom in an elevated position unless the equipment is specifically designed for this use. If allowable, check for overhead power lines and other obstructions in path of travel.*

*Figura 48. Siempre párese en el piso de la canasta. **No** se siente ni se suba a la orilla de la canasta, ni se empine sobre los barandales ni se salga de la canasta. **No** utilice escaleras ni otros objetos para aumentar el alcance. Asegúrese de que el elevador aéreo se opere sobre una superficie nivelada y firme.*

*Figura 49. **No** traslade un elevador aéreo con la pluma en la posición izada a menos que el equipo esté diseñado específicamente para ese fin. Si está permitido moverlo, revise que no haya líneas eléctricas aéreas ni otras obstrucciones en el paso del elevador.*

NOTE: Maintain at least 10-foot distance from overhead power lines.

☑ **Do not** modify the aerial lift equipment in any way unless the manufacturer has approved in writing a specific modification to the equipment.

*Figure 50. Lift controls shall be tested each day prior to use to determine that such controls are in safe working condition. **Do not** exceed the boom and basket safe load limit specified by the manufacturer.*

NOTA: Mantenga una distancia mínima de 10 pies de cualquier cable eléctrico aéreo.

☑ **No** modifique el equipo del elevador aéreo de ninguna manera, a menos que el fabricante haya aprobado por escrito una modificación específica del equipo.

*Figura 50. Los controles del elevador se deberán probar el día antes de usarlos para determinar que están en buen estado de funcionamiento. **No** exceda el límite de carga de la pluma y de la canasta especificado por el fabricante.*

*Figure 51. Field-designed personnel platform for a rough terrain forklift is permitted only if the machine supporting the personnel platform was designed for that purpose, and both the machine and platform meet the requirements for capacity, construction, access, use, and fall protection, including attaching the entire platform to the fork and ensuring the forklift is **not** moved horizontally while the platform is occupied.*

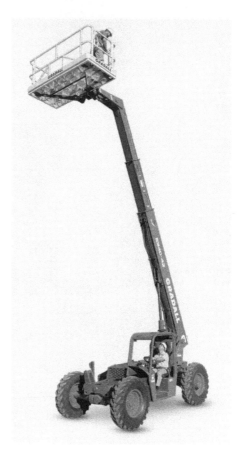

*Figura 51. No se permite improvisar o diseñar en la obra una plataforma para los trabajadores. A veces el fabricante diseñará una plataforma para un elevador de horquilla específico, y certificará que dicha plataforma se puede usar si se usa de acuerdo con sus especificaciones sobre capacidad, construcción, acceso, uso, protección contra caídas, y la manera de unir la plataforma al elevador de horquilla y asegurar que la horquilla **No** se mueva horizontalmente mientras la plataforma está ocupada.*

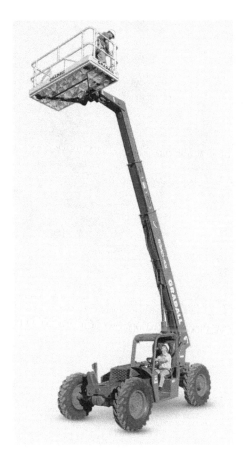

Figure 52. Homemade boxes lifted by a folklift are not acceptable.

Figura 52. Cajas domésticamente fabricadas levantadas por un elavedor de horquilla no son aceptables.

Appendix A

COMPETENT PERSON SCAFFOLD INSPECTION CHECKLIST

Project: _____

Address: _____

Contractor: _____

Date of Inspection: _____ Inspector: _____

	Yes	No	Action/Comments
1. Are scaffolds and scaffold components inspected before each shift by a competent person?			
2. Has competent person been in charge of erection?			
3. Have employees who use the scaffold been trained by a qualified person to recognize the hazards associated with this scaffold and know the performance of their duties relating to it?			
4. Is the load on the scaffold (including point loading) within the maximum load capacity of this particular scaffold and communicated to all employees?			
5. Are scaffold components and planking in safe condition for use (free of visible defects) and plank graded for scaffold use?			
6. Do planks have minimum 12 inches overlap and extend at least 6 inches and no more than 12 inches over the supports?			
7. Are all working platforms fully planked?			
8. Is the scaffold on base plates and is the mudsills level, sound, and rigid?			
9. Have screw jacks (scaffold feet) been used to level and plumb scaffold instead of unstable objects such as concrete blocks, loose bricks, etc.?			
10. Is the scaffold plumb, square, and level?			
11. Is the scaffold secured (tied or guyed) according to manufacturers recommendations or 4:1 (height to width) secured to a structure at intervals not to exceed 30 feet horizontally and 26 feet vertically to prevent movement of the scaffold?			
12. Is there safe access to all scaffold platforms?			
13. Is guard railing in place on all open sides and ends above 10' (Toprails 39" to 45") and are midrails installed at a height approximately midway between the top edge of the guardrail system and the platform surface.			

	Yes	No	Action/Comments
14. Are toeboards installed properly?			
15. Are all scaffold legs fully braced?			
16. Is the scaffold free of makeshift devices (buckets, boxes, barrels, etc.) or ladders to increase height?			
17. Have hazardous conditions been provided for: Power lines? Wind loading? Possible washout of footing?			
18. Have brackets and accessories been properly placed: Outriggers? All brace connections secured/pinned? Frames locked together with stacking pins to prevent uplift?			

Appendix B

SCAFFOLDING WORK SURFACES

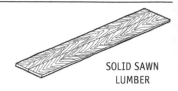

LAMINATED
VENEER LUMBER
(LVL)

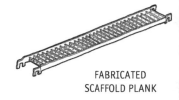

SOLID SAWN
LUMBER

SCAFFOLD PLANKS

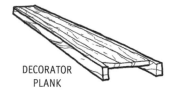

FABRICATED
SCAFFOLD
DECK

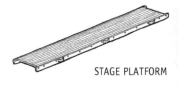

FABRICATED
SCAFFOLD PLANK

DECORATOR
PLANK

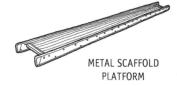

STAGE PLATFORM

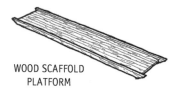

WOOD SCAFFOLD
PLATFORM

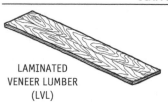

METAL SCAFFOLD
PLATFORM

Appendix C

Grade stamp courtesy of Southern Pine Inspection Bureau

Grade stamp courtesy of West Coast Lumber Inspection Bureau

Glossary

body harness—a design of straps which may be secured about the employee in a manner to distribute the fall arrest forces over at least the thighs, pelvis, waist and shoulders, with means for attaching it to other components of a personal fall arrest system.

brace—a rigid connection that holds one scaffold member in a fixed position with respect to another member, or to a building or structural walls.

cleat—a structural block used at the end of a platform to prevent the platform from slipping off its supports. Cleats are also used to provide footing on sloped surfaces such as crawling boards.

competent person—one who is capable of identifying existing and predictable hazards in the surroundings or working conditions which are unsanitary, hazardous, or dangerous to employees, and who has authorization to take prompt corrective measures to eliminate them.

exposed power lines—electrical power lines which are accessible to employees and which are not shielded from contact. Such lines do not include extension cords or power tool cords.

fabricated frame scaffold (tubular welded frame scaffold)—a scaffold consisting of a platform(s) supported on fabricated end frames with integral posts, horizontal bearers, and intermediate members.

form scaffold—a supported scaffold consisting of a platform supported by brackets attached to formwork.

guardrail system—a vertical barrier, consisting of, but not limited to, toprails, midrails, and posts, erected to prevent employers from falling off a scaffold platform or walkway to lower levels.

lifeline—a component consisting of a flexible line that connects to an anchorage at one end to hang vertically (vertical lifeline), or that connects to anchorages at both ends to stretch horizontally (horizontal lifeline), and which serves as a means for connecting other components of a personal fall arrest system to the anchorage.

lower levels—areas below the level where the employee is located and to which an employee can fall. Such areas include, but are not limited to, ground levels, floors, roofs, ramps, runways, excavations, pits, tanks, materials, water, and equipment.

personal fall arrest system (PFAS)—a system used to stop an employee's fall. It consists of an anchorage, connectors, body harness, and may include a lanyard, deceleration device, lifeline, or combinations of these.

scaffold—any temporary elevated platform (supported or suspended) and its supporting structure (including points of anchorage), used for supporting employees or materials or both.